STARTING TECHNOLOGY

WHEELS

John Williams

**Illustrated by
Malcolm S. Walker**

Wayland

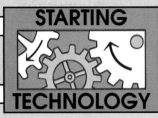

Titles in this series

AIR
FLIGHT
MACHINES
TIME
WATER
WHEELS

Words printed in **bold** appear in the glossary on page 30

© Copyright 1990 Wayland (Publishers) Ltd

First published in 1990 by
Wayland (Publishers) Ltd
61 Western Road, Hove
East Sussex BN3 1JD, England

Editor: Anna Girling
Designer: Kudos Design Services

British Library Cataloguing in Publication Data
Williams, John
  Wheels.
  1. Wheels
  I. Title II. Series
  621.811
ISBN 1 85210 984 X

Typeset by Kudos Editorial and Design Services, Sussex, England
Printed in Italy by Rotolito Lombarda S.p.A.
Bound in Belgium by Casterman S.A.

CONTENTS

ROLLERS

Long ago, people did not know about wheels. If they needed to move very big loads, they had to pull them along the ground. To make it easier, they used to put several round poles under the load. Sometimes, the poles needed to be as large as tree trunks. The **Ancient Egyptians** used rollers like this to move the giant stones which they needed to build the **pyramids**.

This boat is being pulled up the beach on rollers.

4

Using rollers

You will need:

Some round sticks, such as
  garden canes or pencils
String
A brick
A spring balance

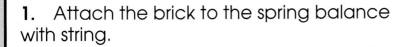

1. Attach the brick to the spring balance
with string.

2. Pull the brick along the floor by holding
the ring on the end of the spring balance.
Do not put the sticks under the brick yet.

3. Look at the marker on the **scale** of the
spring balance and write down the number.

4. Now put the sticks under the brick and try
pulling it along the floor again. Is the marker
at the same place on the balance as
before? Is it higher up or lower down the
scale? Did the brick feel easier to move?

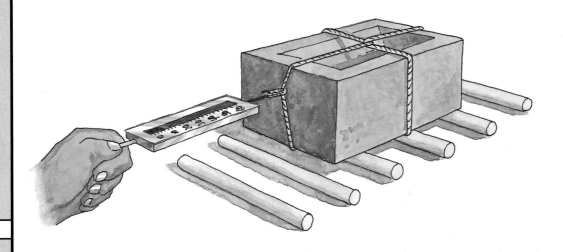

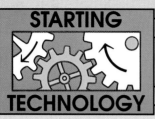

WHEEL IDEAS

Some people say that the wheel is the greatest **invention** ever. Wheels must have made life easier for everyone. Imagine a world without wheels. How could we carry all the big, heavy loads from one town to another? There would be no cars, no trains, no lorries, no bicycles — and no skateboards!

This girl's roller skates have wide, round wheels.

Different kinds of wheels

Make a collection of different things that you think will make good wheels. Here are some ideas to start with.

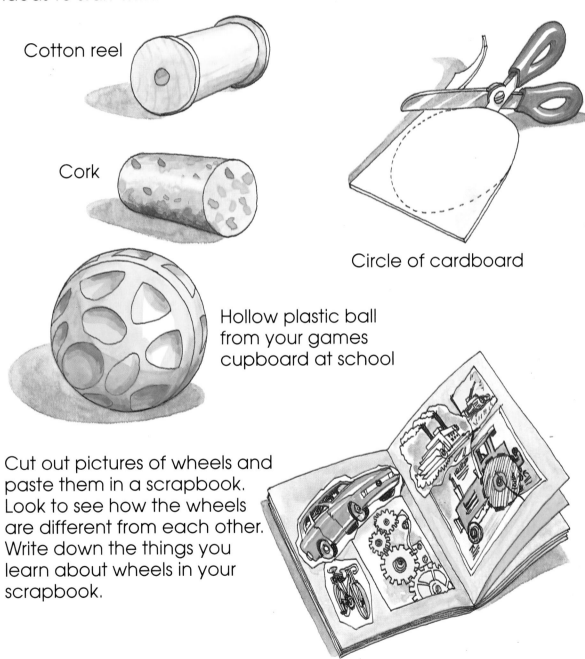

Cotton reel

Cork

Circle of cardboard

Hollow plastic ball from your games cupboard at school

Cut out pictures of wheels and paste them in a scrapbook. Look to see how the wheels are different from each other. Write down the things you learn about wheels in your scrapbook.

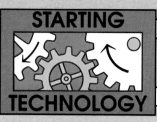

SIMPLE CARTS

Making a simple cart

You will need:

A shallow cardboard box
Some card
Scissors
Four paper fasteners

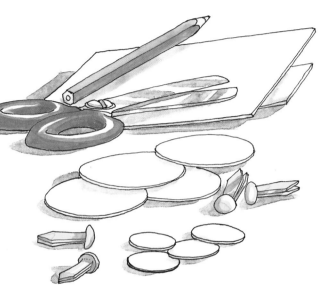

1. Cut out four circles, all the same size, from the card. Also cut out four smaller circles.

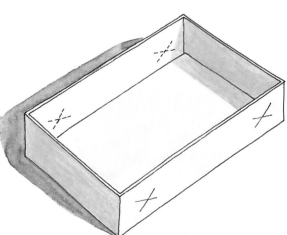

2. On one side of the box, mark the place where you will fix two of the wheels. Do the same on the opposite side of the box. Make sure your wheels will line up, otherwise your cart will wobble.

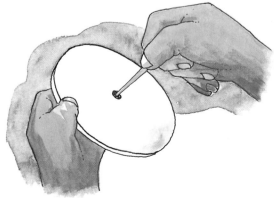

3. Make a neat hole in the middle of the large cardboard wheels, big enough for them to spin round on the paper fasteners.

4. Push a paper fastener through a small cardboard circle, then through one of your cardboard wheels, and lastly through the side of the box. Open up the fastener so that it does not fall out.

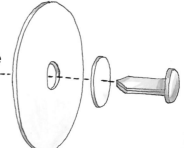

5. Attach all four wheels in this way.

This go-kart has four wheels, one at each corner, like the model cart you can make.

AXLES

The wheels that you made for the cart on page 8 were not joined together. Most wheels used on carts, trains, cars and lorries have axles. An axle is a kind of rod that can join two wheels together so that they turn round at the same time.

Not all wheels need long axles. These racing cars do have axles, but they are very short and are fixed in position separately.

Making pairs of wheels with axles

Type One

You will need:

Two cardboard circles
A cocktail stick
Glue

1. Use the cardboard circles as wheels. Push the stick through the centre of the wheels.

2. Keep the wheels in place with glue.

Type Two

You will need:

Two cotton reels
A short piece of garden cane
Four pieces of plastic tube about
  1 cm long

1. Put the cotton reels on each end of the garden cane axle, with a piece of plastic tube on either side to keep them in place. Make sure the reels can spin round easily.

2. If you cannot find any plastic tube, try winding rubber bands tightly round the axle instead.

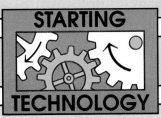

TROLLEYS

Making a simple trolley with axles

You will need:

A small cardboard box
Two wooden manicure sticks
  (you can buy these from a
  chemist's shop)
Four cardboard wheels
Glue
A plank of wood

1. Make two holes on one side of the cardboard box. Do the same on the opposite side.

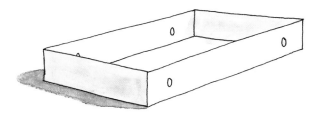

2. Push the sticks through the holes. The holes should be slightly wider than the sticks.

3. Push a cardboard wheel on to each end of the sticks. Make sure the sticks go through the centre of the wheels. Use a little glue to keep them on. The axles should be fixed at **right angles** to the box.

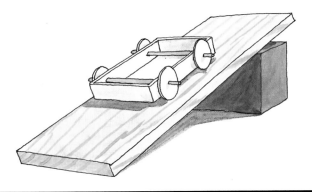

4. Prop up one end of the plank to make a slope. Test your trolley by letting it run down the slope.

Further work

Make a trolley with its axles and
wheels fixed at different angles.
Test your trolley on the slope.
Does it run down like the first
trolley?

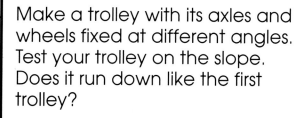

Fix different sets of wheels on to your trolley.
Cut out pieces of card of different shapes.
Here are some suggestions.

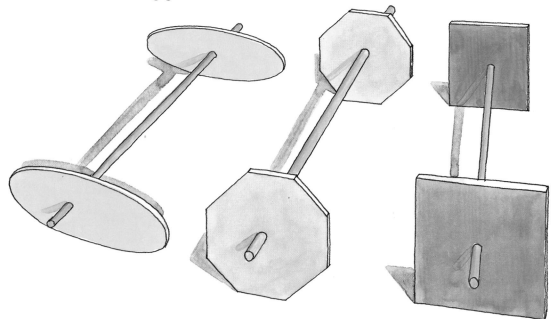

Try these different wheels on your slope. Do
they work as well as round wheels?

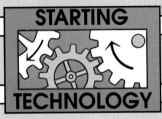
MORE TROLLEYS

Making a better trolley

You will need:

A piece of balsawood about 20 cm long and 10 cm wide
Two pieces of garden cane
Two rubber bands
Four cotton reels
Eight pieces of plastic tube about 1cm long

1. Fix the garden cane axles on to the piece of wood with rubber bands. Use one rubber band for each axle.

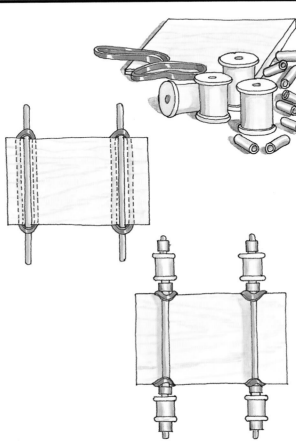

2. Slide pieces of plastic tube on to each end of the axles.

3. Now slide the four cotton reels on to the axles.

4. Fix the other four pieces of plastic tube on to the ends of the axles. If you do not have any plastic tube, wind rubber bands tightly around the axles instead.

Further work

Test your trolley by letting it run down a slope made from a plank of wood. Always let the trolley run down the slope from the same place on the plank. How far does the trolley go?

Change the slope of your plank. Does the trolley travel the same distance if the slope is different?

Put some plasticine on the trolley. How far does it travel now?

Skateboards will always run down slopes, but they can also travel a long way on flat ground. This is because their wheels turn smoothly.

INSECT TROLLEYS

Insects such as ants, butterflies, beetles and bugs all have six legs. You can turn the trolley you made on page 14 into an insect with six wheels instead of legs.

This beetle is a kind of insect. Can you see its six legs?

Making a toy insect

You will need:

Your trolley (see page 14)
Two more cotton reels
Another piece of garden
  cane
A rubber band

Plastic tubes
Some card
A pipe cleaner
Glue
Paints

1. Use the garden cane, cotton reels, plastic tubes and rubber band to fix another set of wheels to your trolley — just as shown on page 14.

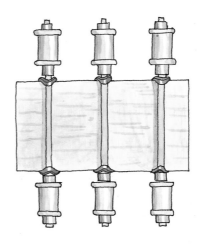

2. Cut out the shape of an insect from card. Glue it to your trolley.

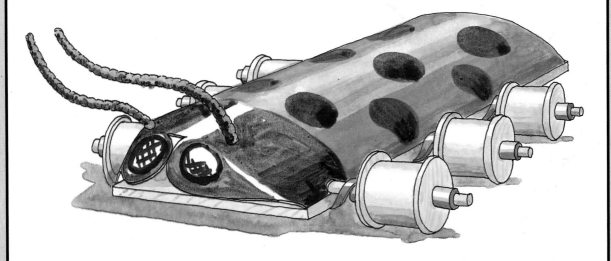

3. Paint your insect and make the **antennae** out of the pipe cleaner.

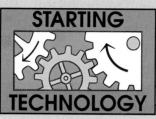

PASSENGERS

People use wheels to help them get around. Perhaps you use wheels yourself. Maybe you go to school every day in a bus or car. Trains, buses and cars have seats for **passengers** to sit down. Cars also have **safety belts**.

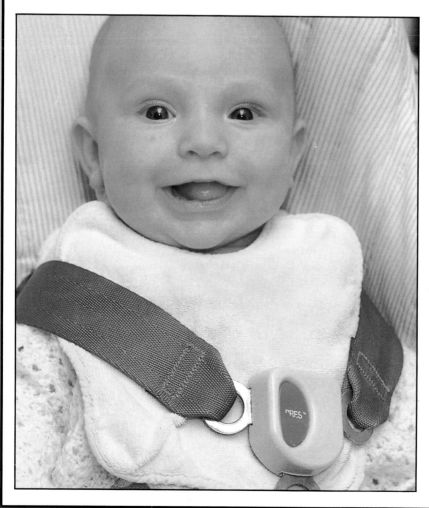

This small child is wearing a special seat belt for babies.

Making a seat for a passenger

You will need:

Your trolley (see page 14)
Plasticine and pipe cleaners
A plank of wood
Pens and paper

Squared paper
Rubber bands
Card
Glue

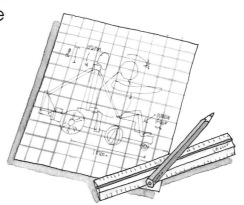

1. Make a model passenger out of plasticine and pipe cleaners.

2. Think about making a seat for your model. How will it be fixed to the trolley? How will the passenger stay in the seat? Write down your ideas.

3. Draw a plan on squared paper of the seat you are going to make. Use this as a **pattern** and make the seat out of card. Fix the seat to the trolley using glue or rubber bands.

4. Put the passenger in the seat. Make a safety belt for your passenger from rubber bands.

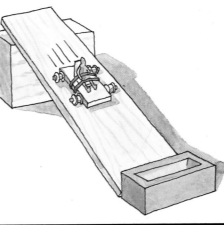

5. Put a brick at the bottom of the slope. What happens to the passenger when the trolley hits the brick. Now try without the safety belt. What happens?

Making a rubber-band buggy

You will need:

A plastic washing-up liquid bottle
A small plastic bead
Some stiff wire

A strong rubber band
A short piece of garden cane
A cork

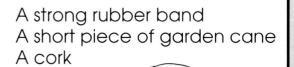

1. Make a small hole in the bottom of the plastic bottle and push the rubber band through it. Stop the band from slipping right through with the piece of cane.

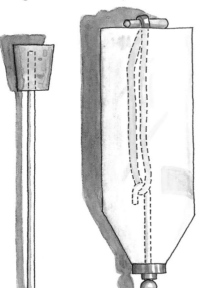

2. Remove the nozzle from the bottle. Put the wire through the bead and then the nozzle. Bend the end of the wire into a hook. Catch the rubber band on the hook and replace the nozzle.

3. Bend the wire at right angles in two places. For safety, put a cork on the end of the wire.

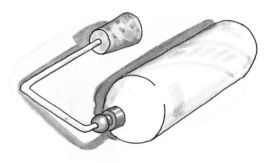

4. Wind up the rubber band by turning the wire around the bottle. Put your buggy on the floor and watch it move.

Further work

You can make a mini merry-go-round out of your buggy. Make a fairground horse out of coloured card and fix it to the free end of the wire. Hold the plastic bottle upright. Wind up the rubber band by turning the wire around the bottle. Let it go and watch the horse spin round.

You cannot see any wheels on this merry-go-round. Do you think it has any wheels underneath to help it spin round?

21

COGWHEELS

Some wheels go round but do not move along. **Cogwheels** are special wheels which help machines work. You can find cogwheels in old clocks and watches. Some cogwheels are connected by special chains. You can see this kind on a bicycle, between the pedals and the back wheel.

Bicycles have cogwheels. They are connected to each other by a chain. If you have a bicycle, look to see which cogwheel is bigger. Is it the one by the pedals or the one on the back wheel?

Making cogwheels

You will need:

Card
Paper fasteners
Glue
A hacksaw

Lollipop sticks or
   wooden spatulas
Scissors

1. Cut some lollipop sticks or spatulas in half with the hacksaw. You will need about ten pieces.

2. Cut out a circle from card.

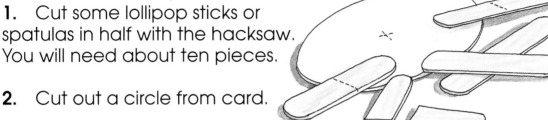

3. Lay the pieces of wood on the circle of card. Their corners should just touch each other at the centre. Glue them to the card.

4. Now make a smaller cogwheel in the same way. You will not need so many pieces of wood.

5. Push paper fasteners through the centres of the cogwheels and attach them to a large piece of thick card. They should just be able to touch each other.

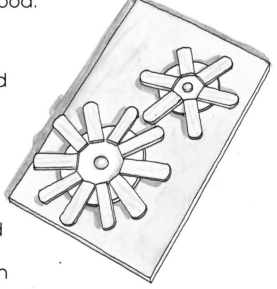

6. Move one cogwheel round. See how it makes the other one move. Move the big wheel round one whole turn. Does the small cogwheel move round more than one turn?

WATER WHEELS

Water wheels have been used for thousands of years. They are usually large wheels with paddles, or flaps, around them. Running water in a river or stream moves the paddles and makes the wheel turn. This movement can then be used to make machinery work.

This old water wheel was used to pump out water from underground mines, to stop them flooding.

Making a simple water wheel

You will need:

Two spatulas or lollipop sticks
A short piece of garden cane
A rubber band
A cotton reel
A hacksaw
Plastic tubes

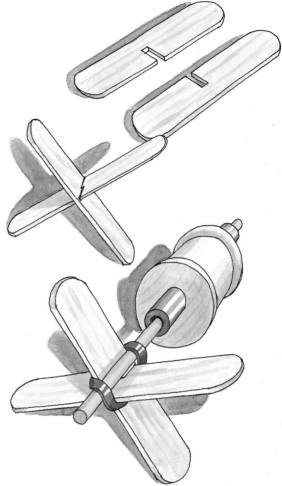

1. Cut a small notch half-way along each spatula. The notches should reach about half-way across. Slot the spatulas into each other.

2. Fix the spatulas on to the end of the cane with a rubber band. Slide the cotton reel on to the other end, with small pieces of plastic tube on either side to hold it in place.

3. Hold the water wheel under a tap in the sink. You should hold on to the cotton reel so that the wheel can spin freely.

4. Slowly turn on the tap. How fast does it need to run before the water wheel begins to spin?

LIFTING A LOAD

Making a water wheel that will lift a load

You will need:

Two plastic bottles	A cotton reel
Rubber bands	Plasticine
String	A stand
Two pieces of garden cane	A clamp

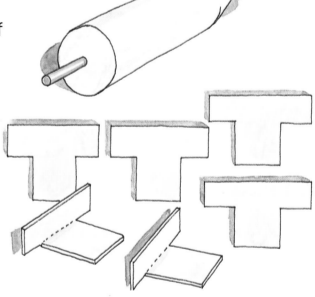

1. Make a hole at the end of one of the bottles and push a piece of cane through until it comes out of the neck. Make sure the bottle can spin freely.

2. Cut out six T-shaped pieces from the other plastic bottle. Fold up the 'stem' of each T-shape so that it sticks out.

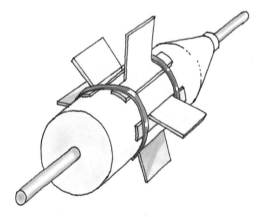

3. Fix the six pieces round the bottle with the rubber bands.

4. Hold each end of the cane and put the water wheel under the tap. How fast does the tap need to run to make the wheel spin?

5. Make a **pulley** by putting a garden cane through a cotton reel. Use a stand and **clamp** to set up the pulley next to the sink.

6. Tie a piece of string to your water wheel and pass it over the cotton reel pulley.

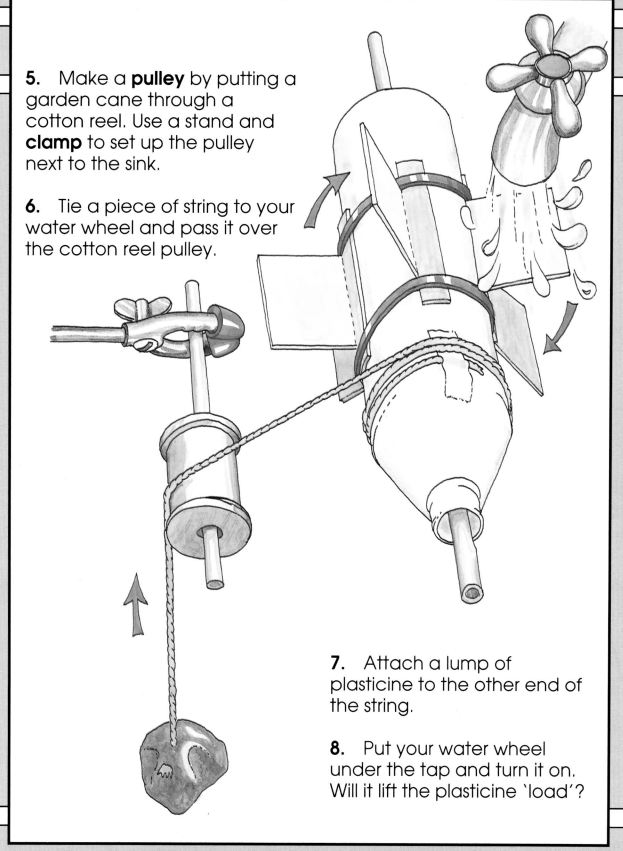

7. Attach a lump of plasticine to the other end of the string.

8. Put your water wheel under the tap and turn it on. Will it lift the plasticine 'load'?

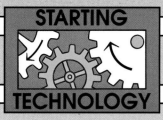

DESIGN AND TECHNOLOGY

All the models in this book have, at one time or another, actually been made by young children. The degree of help needed depends on the individual child.

Often, when children are working in groups, some of them develop specialized skills. In this way, one child can be in charge of sawing, another can do the fixing together, and yet another can do the drawing. In this way, they can all contribute to the model and all feel equally involved.

Children should be encouraged to develop their own ideas and improve on the basic designs in this book. The section on designing a passenger seat gives an introduction to the design process.

Safety should be stressed at all times. Hacksaws and scissors are the tools recommended and, when properly used, are quite safe. Balsawood knives are **not** recommended.

SCIENCE

Although this book is based on simple technology, children will discover the scientific principles involved in work on wheels as they make the various models. By testing their models they will learn about scientific experiments and about recording their results.

HISTORY

Any study of the wheel should involve the history of transport. Children should learn how early civilizations moved loads without wheels. Water wheels can also be studied in a historical context.

MATHEMATICS

All testing involves measurement, often of distance, time or speed, and therefore uses basic mathematics. The recording of these tests can involve making scale diagrams, graphs and charts.

LANGUAGE

Language skills should develop from discussion of activities. Children can also write about their work, but should be encouraged to do so in imaginative as well as descriptive ways.

National Curriculum Attainment Targets

This book is relevant to the following Attainment Targets in the National Curriculum for science:

Attainment Target 1 (Exploration of science) The construction, development and testing of the models throughout this book is relevant. Particular attention should be paid to the development of a fair test (level 3).

Attainment Target 10 (Forces) Any of the models that are moved by a push or a pull involve forces. The movement may be caused by a mechanical device, the child's body, or the force of gravity. Where models have moving parts, the force of friction is involved.

Attainment Target 13 (Energy) Energy is involved in all these models – kinetic, mechanical or potential.

The following Attainment Targets are involved to a lesser extent:

Attainment Target 2 (The variety of life) When making the wheeled insect children will have the chance to study animal life.

Attainment Target 6 (Types and uses of materials) Children will need to experience the properties of different materials when choosing them for the various models.

Attainment Target 12 (Information technology) Children should be encouraged to record their work using computers.

Teachers should be aware of the Attainment Targets covered in other National Curriculum documents – that is, those for design and technology, mathematics, history and language.

GLOSSARY

Ancient Egyptians   The people who lived in Egypt about 4,500 years ago.

Antennae   The feelers that stick out from the heads of insects and other small animals.

Clamp   A piece of equipment that grips an object and holds it in place.

Cogwheels   Wheels that have teeth round the outside.

Insects   Tiny creatures that have six legs.

Invention   The discovery of a new machine which is very useful.

Passengers   The people travelling in a car, bus or train, except the driver.

Pattern   A design that you can copy in order to make something.

Pulley   A wheel with a rope round it, used for lifting heavy objects.

Pyramids   The large, triangular, pointed buildings that the Ancient Egyptians made to hold the body of a dead king or queen.

Right angle   An angle is a corner where two lines meet. A right angle is a square corner, like the corner of a book or box.

Safety belts   The straps in cars which passengers and drivers do up round them to hold them safely in their seats.

Scale   A line of regular marks used for measuring.

BOOKS TO READ

All About Wheels   by Ali Mitgutsch (Dent, 1985)
Big Wheels   by Anne Rockwell (Hamish Hamilton, 1986)
Fun with Wheels   by Ed Catherall (Wayland, 1986)
Wheels   by Bob Graham (Blackie, 1986)

Picture acknowledgements
The publishers would like to thank the following for allowing their photographs to be reproduced in this book: Cephas Picture Library 22; Eye Ubiquitous 21; Chris Fairclough Colour Library 6, 10, 18; Oxford Scientific Films 16; PHOTRI 15; Topham 4, 9; Zefa 24. Cover photography by Zul Mukhida.